Recycle,
Reduce,
Reuse,
Rethink

Household Waste

Kate Walker

Smart Apple Media

This edition first published in 2005 in the United States of America by Smart Apple Media.

Smart Apple Media
1980 Lookout Drive
North Mankato
Minnesota 56003

Library of Congress Cataloging-in-Publication Data

Walker, Kate.
  Household waste / by Kate Walker.
  p. cm. — (Recycle, reduce, reuse, rethink)
  Includes index.
  ISBN 1-58340-561-5 (alk. paper)
  1. Refuse and refuse disposal—Juvenile literature.
  2. Recycling (Waste, etc.)—Juvenile literature. I. Title. II. Series.

  TD792.W34 2004
  363.72'88—dc22   2003070386

First Edition
9 8 7 6 5 4 3 2 1

First published in 2004 by
MACMILLAN EDUCATION AUSTRALIA PTY LTD
627 Chapel Street, South Yarra, Australia, 3141

Associated companies and representatives throughout the world.

Edited by Helena Newton
Text and cover design by Cristina Neri, Canary Graphic Design
Technical illustrations and cartoons by Vaughan Duck
Photo research by Legend Images

Printed in China

Acknowledgements
The author and the publisher are grateful to the following for permission to reproduce
copyright material:

Cover photograph: San Mateo Landfill, near Manila, Philippines, courtesy of Reuters.

NHPA/ANTphoto.com, p. 22; John Cancalosi/Auscape International, p. 12; Yves Lanceau/Auscape
International, p. 15; Digital Vision, p. 19; Getty News, p. 9; Great Southern Stock, pp. 16, 17; GreenPC,
p. 24; Wade Hughes/Lochman Transparencies, p. 13; Dennis Sarson/Lochman Transparencies, p. 8;
Merlin, Re~Cycle, p. 26 (both); Photodisc, p. 5 & design features; Sharon Purchase, pp. 25 (both), 29;
Dale Mann/Retrospect, p. 23; Reuters, pp. 11, 18; Slim Your Bin, Cambridgeshire Council, p. 20; Mark
Edwards/Still Pictures, p. 21; The G.R. "Dick" Roberts Photo Library, p. 14; Jan Willem den Besten, p. 27.

While every care has been taken to trace and acknowledge copyright, thepublisher tenders their
apologies for any accidental infringement where copyright has proved untraceable. Where the attempt
has been unsuccessful, the publisher welcomes information that would redress the situation.

Contents

Let's start recycling now!

When a word is printed in **bold**, you can look up its meaning in the glossary on page 31.

Recycling

Recycling means using products and materials again to make new products instead of throwing them away.

Why recycle?

Developed countries have become known as "throw-away societies" because they use and throw away so many products, often after just one use! Single-use products include drink cans, glass jars, sheets of paper, and plastic bags. Today, there are approximately six billion people in the world. By the year 2050, there could be as many as nine billion people. The world's population is growing fast, and people are using a lot more products and materials than they did in the past.

Instead of throwing products away, we can recycle them. When we recycle:

- we use fewer of the Earth's **natural resources**
- manufacturing is "greener" because recycling creates less **pollution** than using **raw materials**
- we reduce waste, which is better for the environment.

Governments, industries, communities, and individuals all around the world are finding different ways to solve the problems of how to conserve resources, reduce manufacturing pollution and waste, and protect the environment. If the Earth is to support nine billion people in the future, it is important that we all start recycling now!

As well as recycling, we can:

- reduce the number of products and materials we use
- reuse products and materials
- rethink the way we use products and materials.

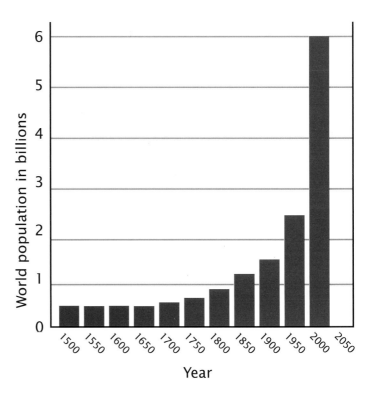

Today, there are more people on Earth using more products and materials than in the past, and the population is still growing.

What is household waste?

Household waste is all the things that families and other people living in households throw away.

The history of household waste

Before the 1950s, household waste was made up of dirty papers, rags, food cans, food scraps, and ash from fireplaces. Drink bottles were never thrown away. They were returned to the drink manufacturer and refilled. Most papers were saved for other uses. Glass jars were saved and used to store things. Clothes were mended, and broken toys and furniture were repaired.

In the 1950s, life changed for people in developed countries. Hundreds of new products were invented, including cheap plastic goods. Some products became so cheap they could be thrown away after just one use. At the same time, people began to earn more money and used it to buy more things. This new wealth and these new inventions created a lot more waste.

Household waste today

Today, household waste is made up of:
- 35 percent food scraps and plant waste
- 25 percent paper
- 17 percent plastics
- 9 percent glass
- 7.8 percent steel
- 4 percent dust
- 2.2 percent aluminum.

These percentages show the **volume**, or amount of space, that each type of household waste takes up.

Households in developed countries produce mountains of waste.

How household waste

Some household waste is buried in **landfills** and some is recycled. The average household in a developed country throws away 1,005 pounds (456 kg) of **organic waste**, 514 pounds (233 kg) of paper, 141 pounds (64 kg) of plastics, 134 pounds (61 kg) of glass, 62 pounds (28 kg) of steel, and 18 pounds (8 kg) of aluminum each year.

The household waste that is recycled goes through several processes.

People recycle food and plant waste, or organic waste, at home. They turn it into **compost** and use it to **fertilize** soil.

People put recyclable materials into one or more different bins for curbside collection.

1

Recyclable materials are taken to a recycling center and sorted into **pure streams** of the same type of material.

2

3

Each pure-stream material is put into a large bundle, called a bale, or into a bin and taken to the **reprocessing plant**.

is recycled

6 New products made from recycled materials are bought by consumers.

5 The cleaned material is melted or **pulped** and made into new products.

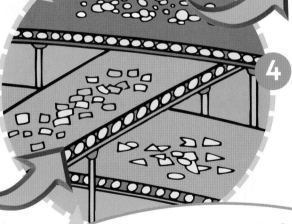

4 At the reprocessing plant, each pure-stream material is broken into small pieces and cleaned.

1,005 pounds (456 kg) of organic waste = 130 buckets of food scraps

514 pounds (233 kg) of paper = 1,165 newspapers

141 pounds (64 kg) of plastics = 1,828 empty 1-liter bottles

134 pounds (61 kg) of glass = 172 empty half-liter glass bottles

62 pounds (28 kg) of steel = 1,273 empty steel cans

18 pounds (8 kg) of aluminum = 571 empty aluminum cans

Recycled household

Household waste is recycled in two ways: through a closed- or an open-loop cycle. The end products made from different types of recycled household waste depend on the kind of loop they go through.

A closed-loop cycle

Closed-loop recycling

Closed-loop recycling happens when used materials are remade into new products again and again. The materials go round in a non-stop loop and are never wasted.

Closed-loop household waste products

Some household waste products that can be recycled in a closed loop are:

↻ *fruit and vegetable scraps* These **decompose** into compost and are used to fertilize soil to grow more fruit and vegetables.

↻ *used white paper* This is made into new white paper.

↻ *used cardboard* This is made into new cardboard.

↻ *used plastic bottles* These are melted to make new plastic bottles.

↻ *used glass bottles and jars* These are ground up and added to molten (melted) glass to make new bottles and jars.

↻ *used steel food and drink cans* These are melted to make new food and drink cans.

↻ *used aluminum cans* These are melted to make new aluminum cans.

Vegetables grow well in soil fertilized with compost.

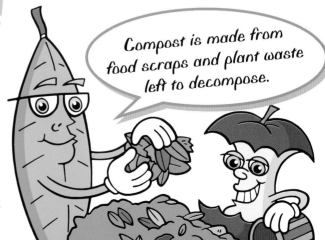

Compost is made from food scraps and plant waste left to decompose.

waste products

Open-loop recycling

Open-loop recycling happens when used materials are made into products that cannot be recycled again. The materials are reused only once and then thrown away. Many people believe this is not recycling at all because the materials are wasted.

Open-loop household waste products

Some household waste products that can be recycled in an open loop are:

- ♻ **used paper**   This is made into bathroom tissues. Tissues cannot be recycled because they are **contaminated** waste.

- ♻ **used plastic bottles**   These are melted to make fibers for clothes, sleeping-bag filler, and webbing for seatbelts. These products cannot be recovered in large, pure streams. At the end of their life, most are thrown away.

- ♻ **used plastic and glass**   These are bonded together to make a tough material called fiberglass. Fiberglass cannot be recycled because the plastic and glass cannot be separated again.

- ♻ **mixed plastic waste**   This is melted to make plastic park benches and crash barriers for roads. These products last for many years, but cannot be recycled because they cannot be collected in large, clean quantities.

- ♻ **mixed household waste containing a lot of plastic and paper**   This is burned as fuel to generate electricity. The ash left over is buried in landfills.

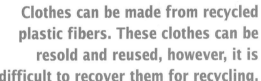

Clothes can be made from recycled plastic fibers. These clothes can be resold and reused, however, it is difficult to recover them for recycling.

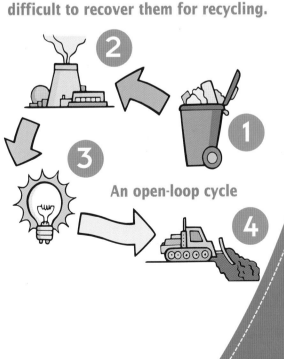

An open-loop cycle

Why recycle

When used household waste products are recycled to make new products:

- ↻ we use fewer of the Earth's natural resources
- ↻ manufacturing is "greener" because recycling creates less pollution than using raw materials
- ↻ we reduce waste, which is better for the environment.

Reasons for recycling organic waste

Recycling organic waste reduces the need to mine and make **inorganic fertilizers** and keeps organic waste out of landfills.

Reasons for recycling	How recycling helps
CONSERVING NATURAL RESOURCES	↻ When organic waste is recycled into compost and used as a fertilizer, inorganic fertilizers can be left in the ground for future use.
"GREENER" MANUFACTURING	↻ When organic waste is recycled into compost, no harmful substances are produced, whereas **refining** inorganic fertilizers produces air pollution.
REDUCING WASTE	↻ Recycling organic waste keeps it out of landfills, where it makes up 35 percent of the total volume.
PROTECTING THE ENVIRONMENT	↻ Recycling organic waste keeps it out of landfills, where it decomposes without oxygen and gives off **methane** gas, which adds to **global warming**. Methane gas also starts landfill fires, causing plastics to burn and release **toxic** substances.

How landfills add to global warming

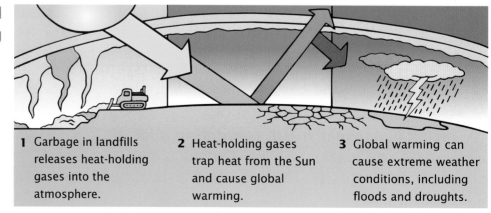

1 Garbage in landfills releases heat-holding gases into the atmosphere.

2 Heat-holding gases trap heat from the Sun and cause global warming.

3 Global warming can cause extreme weather conditions, including floods and droughts.

household waste?

Reasons for recycling paper

Recycling paper saves trees and **fossil fuels**, creates less pollution than making paper from new materials, and reduces the build-up of paper in landfills, which is better for the environment.

Landfill sites use up valuable land that could be used for cities and farms.

Reasons for recycling	How recycling helps
CONSERVING NATURAL RESOURCES	When paper is recycled, more forests are left for future use.
	Making paper from recycled paper pulp uses up to 40 percent less power than making paper from new pulp. Fossil fuels are the main power source for paper making and fossil fuels are **non-renewable** resources.
"GREENER" MANUFACTURING	Making paper from recycled paper pulp uses fewer harsh chemicals than making paper from new pulp, and when paper is recycled, no dangerous chlorine bleach is used.
REDUCING WASTE	Recycling paper keeps it out of landfills, where it makes up 25 percent of the total volume.
PROTECTING THE ENVIRONMENT	When paper is recycled, more trees are left to grow and take **carbon dioxide** out of the atmosphere and turn it into oxygen. Today, too much carbon dioxide in the atmosphere from burning fossil fuels is adding to global warming.
	Recycling paper saves forests, which are the **habitats** of many animals.
	When paper is recycled it is kept out of landfills, where it gives off methane gas, which adds to global warming.

Reasons for recycling plastics

Recycling plastics saves natural resources, reduces manufacturing pollution and waste, and makes the environment safer for people and wildlife.

Reasons for recycling	How recycling helps
CONSERVING NATURAL RESOURCES	When plastics are recycled, less petroleum is used. Petroleum is a fossil fuel and a scarce, non-renewable resource.
"GREENER" MANUFACTURING	Making plastics from recycled material uses fewer dangerous chemicals and up to 70 percent less fuel than making plastics from raw materials. This means there is far less air pollution.
REDUCING WASTE	Recycling plastics keeps them out of landfills, where they make up 17 percent of the total volume.
PROTECTING THE ENVIRONMENT	Recycling plastics reduces the risk of harmful oil spills, because less petroleum needs to be drilled and transported.
	Recycling plastics keeps them out of landfills. This reduces the risk of toxic substances in some plastics being washed by rain into surrounding soil and waterways and contaminating them. It also reduces the risk of toxic gases being given off into the atmosphere by plastics burning in landfill fires.
	When more plastics are recycled, there is less plastic litter around to endanger wildlife.

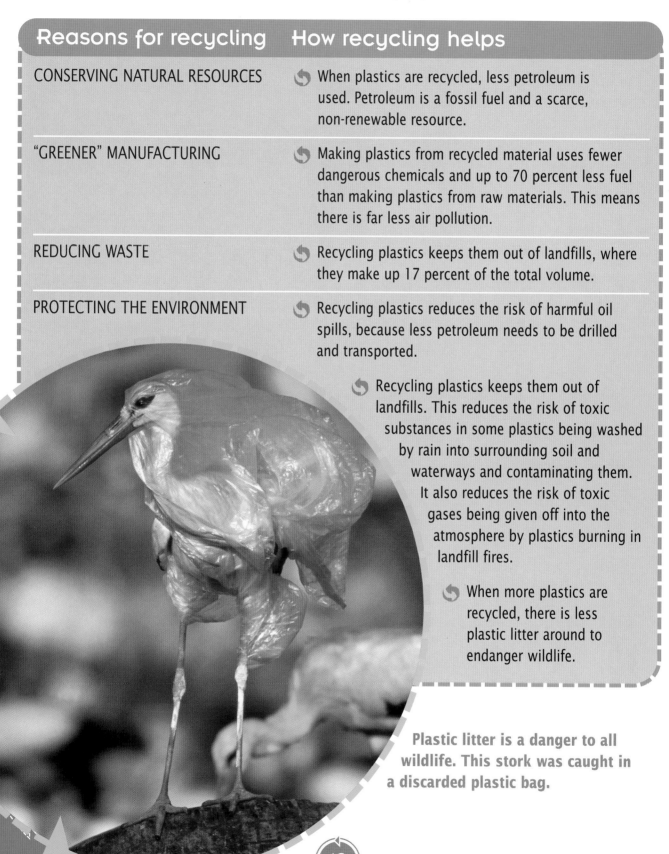

Plastic litter is a danger to all wildlife. This stork was caught in a discarded plastic bag.

Reasons for recycling glass

Recycling glass saves sand deposits and fossil fuels, reduces manufacturing pollution, reduces the build-up of glass in landfills, and saves people and wildlife from harm.

Industries release dangerous gases into the atmosphere, which cause breathing problems for some people.

Reasons for recycling	How recycling helps
CONSERVING NATURAL RESOURCES	When glass is recycled, less sand, soda ash, and lime are used to make new glass. The world has large deposits of these materials and they will last for thousands of years, however, making glass from recycled material uses up to 40 percent fewer fossil fuels than making glass from raw materials. Fossil fuels are scarce, non-renewable resources.
"GREENER" MANUFACTURING	Fossil fuels burned during glass making give off carbon dioxide gas, which adds to global warming, and nitrogen oxide gas, which creates a dangerous form of air pollution called **smog**. When glass is recycled, less carbon dioxide and nitrogen oxide are produced.
REDUCING WASTE	Recycling glass keeps it out of landfills, where it makes up 9 percent of the total volume.
PROTECTING THE ENVIRONMENT	When glass is recycled, less sand, trona, and limestone are mined. Trona is made into soda ash, and limestone into lime, to make glass. Less mining means more plant and animal habitats are left undisturbed.
	When glass is recycled, there is less glass litter around to cause serious cuts or to start wildfires.

Reasons for recycling steel

Recycling steel saves iron ore and coal, reduces manufacturing pollution, and reduces the build-up of steel waste, which is better for the environment.

Reasons for recycling	How recycling helps
CONSERVING NATURAL RESOURCES	When steel is recycled, iron ore and coal are left in the ground for future use. The world's iron ore deposits will last for thousands of years. However, the world's coal deposits could be used up by the year 2400.
"GREENER" MANUFACTURING	Making steel from recycled material uses up to 60 percent less coal than making steel from raw materials. Burning less coal reduces a dangerous form of air pollution called **acid rain**. Acid rain damages plants and takes plant food out of the soil.
REDUCING WASTE	Recycling steel keeps it out of landfills, where it makes up 7.8 percent of the total volume.
PROTECTING THE ENVIRONMENT	When steel is recycled, a lot less coal and iron ore are mined, which means a lot less damage is done to plant and animal habitats and waterways.
	Recycling steel removes steel litter from the environment, where it rusts and pollutes soil and waterways.
	When steel food cans are recycled instead of being thrown away as litter, animals do not risk getting their heads caught inside.

Coal mines can severely damage the environment.

Reasons for recycling aluminum

Recycling aluminum saves bauxite, reduces manufacturing pollution, and reduces the build-up of aluminum waste, which is better for the environment.

The beautiful Karahnukar region of Iceland will be flooded if the Icelandic government builds a planned dam. The dam would supply power for making aluminum.

Reasons for recycling	How recycling helps
CONSERVING NATURAL RESOURCES	↻ When aluminum is recycled, more bauxite is left in the ground for future use. The world's bauxite reserves will last for several hundred years, but they will last longer if aluminum is recycled.
"GREENER" MANUFACTURING	↻ When aluminum is made from recycled material, no harsh caustic soda is needed to dissolve the bauxite, and no dangerous fluoride gases are released into the atmosphere from aluminum refining.
REDUCING WASTE	↻ Recycling aluminum keeps it out of landfills where it makes up 2.2 percent of the total volume.
PROTECTING THE ENVIRONMENT	↻ When aluminum is recycled, less bauxite is mined, and less damage is done to plant and animal habitats.
	↻ Making aluminum from recycled material uses 95 percent less power than making aluminum from raw materials. Most of the power used for aluminum **smelting** comes from **hydro-electric power** plants, which use water from large hydro dams. Hydro dams are often built by flooding whole river valleys and destroying large areas of plant and animal habitats.
	↻ When aluminum is recycled, fewer drink cans are thrown away as litter.

For and against

Answer:

Yes, if people act now to preserve the environment and manage the Earth's resources better.

Question:

Can this be achieved just by recycling?

"YES" The "yes" case for recycling

The world's growing population can be sustained if resources are managed better.

✓ Recycling household waste means that valuable resources are left in the ground for people to use in the future.

✓ Making new products from recycled materials uses less energy, fewer toxic substances, and causes less pollution than making new products from raw materials.

✓ Less mining and less pollution help keep the environment healthy so that it keeps producing the **renewable** resources that people in the future will need. These resources include forests, food crops, and fish.

✓ A lot of materials can be recycled forever and stay just as strong and valuable. These materials include organic waste, plastics, glass, steel, and aluminum.

✓ As more materials are recycled, the recycling process becomes better and cheaper.

Paper and cardboard cannot be recycled forever. After being recycled several times, they become weak and must be thrown away.

recycling

Question:
Do most people agree that recycling is a good idea?

Answer:
Yes.

Question:
Will recycling fix all the problems caused by product manufacturing and waste?

"NO" The "no" case against recycling

✗ Household waste materials are collected by trucks that burn fossil fuels. This means that scarce fossil fuel resources are being used to save less scarce resources, such as those used for paper and glass making.

✗ Recycling is not worthwhile in small towns where only small amounts of materials are generated.

✗ A small amount of contaminating material mixed with a batch of used paper, plastics, aluminum, or glass can prevent it from being recycled. The whole load must be dumped in a landfill.

✗ All recycling processes use up energy and involve some harmful chemicals.

Trucks that collect materials for recycling go slowly from house to house, burning up valuable fossil fuels.

✗ The high cost of sorting household waste sometimes makes recycled materials more expensive than new materials, and people will not buy them.

✗ Some people believe that recycling is solving all the problems of resource use, pollution, and waste. If materials were not being recycled, these people might stop using and wasting them.

Reduce, reuse,

Recycling is a great idea, but it is just one answer to the problems of how to conserve resources, reduce manufacturing pollution and waste, and protect the environment. There are other things we can do that are even better than recycling. We can reduce, reuse, and rethink what we use.

Reduce

The best and quickest way to reduce household waste is to use fewer products! Reducing is easy. Some of the ways you can reduce household waste are to:

↻ buy fewer throw-away products, such as plastic food wrap and paper plates

↻ stop buying products that are not really needed, such as several different magazines and newspapers, cheap toys, and gadgets

↻ buy good quality products that will last a long time, instead of cheap products that break quickly

↻ take cloth bags shopping and refuse plastic shopping bags

↻ mix up drinks and make snacks at home and take them on outings so that bottled drinks and packaged snacks do not have to be bought

↻ buy food and cleaning products in bulk to reduce packing waste

↻ put a "No junk mail please" sign on the mailbox.

Many people in developed countries go shopping just for fun, and buy lots of products they do not need.

rethink

Reuse

A lot of household products and materials can be used again. Some of the ways household products and materials can be reused are:

- glass containers, cookie tins, and plastic food containers can all be used to store other things

- unwanted household goods, such as clothes, toys, kitchenware, and furniture, can be given to charity shops for someone else to use

- writing paper can be used on both sides

- newspapers and magazines can be shared with friends

- refillable bottles can be washed and returned to the shops

- food scraps and plant waste can be composted and returned to the soil to grow more plants.

Shoppers can make a difference when they contact a manufacturer and say they have stopped buying a product because it has too much packaging or is non-recyclable.

Rethink

Everyone can come up with new ideas. Some ideas for changing the way we use household products and materials are:

- governments can encourage people to recycle, reduce, and reuse more through advertizing campaigns

- manufacturers can stop using unnecessary plastic and paper packaging

- shoppers can stop buying non-recyclable products, such as plastic-coated paper and metalized plastic film.

What governments

Governments around the world are finding new and better ways to deal with household waste. They are finding ways to recycle, reduce, reuse, and rethink their use of household waste.

Recycle **Reduce** **Reuse**

Running an information campaign

In the Anglia region of England, each household was throwing away about 1.1 tons (1 t) of garbage a year, or 100 garbage bags. More than 80 percent of that waste was being dumped in landfills. Not anymore. Local government councils banded together, and now run a yearly roadshow called "Slim Your Bin."

The roadshow travels from town to town making people aware of what they can do to recycle, reduce, and reuse more materials. The show is made up of singers, jugglers, and actors. They run competitions, give away free gifts, and put on fun shows for free. Each year the roadshow has a different message. In 2001, the message was "Get composting" and people were shown how to compost organic waste at home. This campaign encouraged people in the Cambridgeshire area to compost 26,786 tons (24,300 t) of organic waste instead of sending it to landfills.

GOVERNMENT APPROVED

Each year the "Slim Your Bin" roadshow gets bigger and visits more towns.

Recycle

Recycling organic waste

Organic waste is messy, smelly, and often attracts pests. In the Catalan region of Spain, the local government was not put off by that. They got residents to seal all organic waste in paper bags and place the bags in special bins. The waste is collected each week and taken to composting depots. The organic waste is spread out in rows, watered, and turned by machines. **Bacteria** in the waste convert it into compost in just 16 weeks. The compost is sold to local farmers. In 2000, Catalonia recycled almost one-third of its organic waste.

A large composting center turns organic waste into valuable compost for fertilizing plants.

GOVERNMENT APPROVED

Rethink

Reclaiming land with waste

In the United States, large areas of land have been poisoned by harmful chemicals left at mine sites. The Environmental Protection Agency is using household waste to make contaminated land safe again. Yard waste collected from homes is turned into compost and special bacteria are added to it. The compost is then dug into old mine sites and the bacteria slowly eat the harmful chemicals. In some places the land has been made safe enough to grow food crops.

What industries are

Industries are getting better at recycling a lot more waste materials.

Browser

Address http//:www.industry-updates.com   back forward home go

Favorites \ History \ Search \ Scrapbook \ Page Holder

Recycling paint

In Nova Scotia, Canada, more than two million cans of paint are sold each year. About one-quarter of the paint is never used. The paint industry in Nova Scotia has set up a special paint recycling program. People can now bring their unused paint to recycling centers. The paint is taken to a recycling plant in Springhill and reprocessed into new paint. The used paint cans are recycled as well. In 2002, the Springhill plant recovered 92,470 gallons (350,000 l) of old paint.

Paint and batteries should be taken to hazardous waste disposal centers and never put into household bins. They cause severe soil, water, and air pollution in landfills.

Recycling shoes

The Nike shoe company in the U.S. takes back old running shoes from its customers. The old shoes are ground up to make a product called Nike Grind. Nike Grind is used to make surfaces for playgrounds, basketball courts, and running tracks. It takes 5,000 shoes to surface one basketball court.

doing

Recycle

Sorting household waste

Visy Recycling centers across Australia receive hundreds of tons of household waste every day. The waste is sorted by a series of high-speed machines.

1 All incoming waste is put into a container that rolls around, called a trommel drum. Holes in the trommel drum let metal, glass, plastic, and milk and juice cartons fall through onto a conveyor belt. The paper remains behind.

2 Magnetized belts snatch up steel objects from the conveyor belt and carry them away. The magnetic force in the belt switches off for a moment, and the steel drops into a collection bin.

Tons of mixed waste materials come into Visy Recycling centers every day to be sorted by its high-speed machines.

3 A machine that can sense light, called an opto-electric machine, fires out a beam of light that finds all of the objects made of different colored glass. The machine triggers a jet of air that blasts the glass objects off the conveyor belt and into the right collection bin.

4 Scanners that can find different kinds of plastic, called X ray and near infra-red scanners, trigger a jet of air that shoots different plastics into different bins.

5 A machine that works like a reverse magnet, called a reverse eddy current machine, creates a reverse magnetic field that pushes the aluminum objects off into a bin.

6 Milk and juice cartons are all that remain.

What communities

Communities of people everywhere are working together toward a goal of zero waste for all kinds of material. They are finding better ways to recycle and reuse household waste.

Your local newspaper

Friday November 7

THE DAILY HERALD

Morning edition

Reuse

Reusing personal computers

Every year, thousands of computers are thrown out as household waste. Computers contain valuable materials, including heat-resistant plastics and high-grade metals. Computers also contain toxic substances that contaminate soil and water around landfill sites. In many countries, computers are not recycled because the materials have to be separated by hand and this is often expensive.

In Victoria, Australia, an organization called Infoxchange Australia has set up a project called GreenPC. Businesses and households donate used computers to GreenPC, who repair them using recycled parts. The workers at GreenPC are people who have been unemployed for a long time. More experienced workers teach them how to repair computers.

Trainees at GreenPC learn to repair computers by reusing old computer parts.

At the end of four months training, GreenPC helps the trainees find full-time work. All of the repaired computers are offered to individuals and community groups who need computers but cannot afford to buy them.

are doing

Recycle

Recycling at school

Many towns and communities in New Zealand are serious about recycling. They want all landfills closed by 2015, and no more products and materials thrown away. Campbells Bay Elementary School in Auckland, New Zealand, is one community school that got very serious about recycling.

In 2001, students ran a competition to get ideas on how to reduce school garbage. Senior students put on a show at an assembly to teach everyone about recycling at school and at home. Bins for recycling plastics and metal waste were set up in the playground and all classrooms got paper recycling bins. Students also wrote to their local city council suggesting that the council start a diaper recycling service at child-care centers and hospitals. A Web site was created to help future pupils learn about recycling.

Campbells Bay Elementary School students, Alice and Sophie, check the jumbo-sized worm farm.

Student recycling monitors now check the recycling bins daily to make sure the right materials are going into the right bins. The school has replaced its small **worm farms** with a jumbo-sized worm farm for recycling all food scraps.

Hamish and Michael collect lunchtime food scraps for the worms.

how exciting – the worms are hungry

GOOD   BAD

What individuals

Individuals everywhere are finding ways to reuse and recycle things that are often thrown away.

Individuals making your planet a better place.

Green Fingers Newsletter

Reusing bicycles

Reuse

When Merlin Matthews was in college in London he was known as Dr. Bike, because he often fixed bicycles for friends. One day a friend asked his advice about setting up a bicycle factory in Haiti. Many people in Haiti had to walk long distances just to get water and food. Matthews had a better idea. He knew that millions of bicycles were rusting away in garages across the United Kingdom. Instead of building a factory in Haiti, he set up Re~Cycle, which is a charity that sends used bicycles, tools, and parts overseas.

In 2001, Merlin Matthews received an award for setting up Re~Cycle.

Children in Mtubatuba, Republic of South Africa, are shown how to repair and look after their Re~Cycle bikes.

Today, Matthews collects thousands of used bikes and ships them to Africa and to countries such as Haiti. The bikes are given to men, women, and children who have no other transportation. Children who once walked 6.8 miles (11 km) each way to school can now get there by bike. Parents who once walked four hours each day to work, now cycle back and forth and spend more time with their families.

are doing

Jan Willem den Besten and green worker Sharuk use a motor rickshaw to collect recyclables in Upper Dharamshala.

Starting a clean-up campaign

Dutchman Jan Willem den Besten came to India at age 21, and was troubled by the amount of litter scattered about the beautiful countryside. In many Indian towns, household waste is dumped in the streets because there are no government dump sites. Den Besten made his home in the town of Upper Dharamshala, which is a settlement for people who have been forced to leave their homes in Tibet. He and the local Tibetan welfare officer started a clean-up campaign. Den Besten and three Tibetan "green workers" went from house to house collecting waste materials.

At first, the local people laughed at him and his plan to recycle waste from every house, hotel, and business in the town.

Today, other Indian towns are doing the same thing. Upper Dharamshala's clean-up campaign now has a team of five "green workers" who collect and clean used plastics, metal, and glass, and sell them to reprocessing plants. They run a "Green Shop" selling local craft goods and homemade jams. The project also has a paper-recycling workshop, where Tibetan people are employed to make beautiful handmade paper products from recycled paper waste.

What you can do

You can do all sorts of activities to help recycle organic waste. You can also get others interested and come up with ideas to stop organic waste from going to landfills. Make a weekly "Organic waste scorecard" for yourself or your class.

What to do:

1 Draw up a scorecard with headings like the one shown below.
2 Write down each time you or your class do something to recycle organic waste.
3 Reward yourself or your class with a green star for each activity that you do.

Organic Waste 3-R scorecard

Recycle	Get others interested	Other things
Made my own worm farm.	Talked Grandpa into spreading his lawn clippings on the garden instead of putting them in the garbage bin and sending them to a landfill.	Held a garage sale and sold used games, toys, and books to raise money to buy a compost bin.
Put a bucket under the sink to collect food scraps for the worms.	Asked my teacher if the school could get a worm farm to recycle lunch scraps.	Used the garage sale money to buy the compost bin.
Ripped up an oily pizza box and put it in the worm farm.	Told Mom it was OK to put used tissues in the worm farm.	Wrote a letter to the council asking if green waste from the local park is made into compost. Answer: Yes, it is!
Used an empty ice cream container to bring home lunch scraps from our day at the beach.		
★★★★★	★★★	★★★★

Get others interested

You can make leaflets or a poster showing simple ways to recycle organic waste. Most people want to recycle their organic waste but are not sure how.

> Worms do not like meat, dairy foods, too much oil, animal droppings, or office paper.

> A bold heading will catch people's attention.

RECYCLING ORGANIC WASTE

How to make a worm farm

1 Find a polystyrene fruit box.
2 Punch half-inch (1-cm) holes in the base and stand the box on four small blocks over a drip tray.
3 Fill the box one-third full with wet shredded newspaper and damp soil.
4 Add about 100 earthworms.
5 Cover the soil and worms with sheets of damp newspaper, and seal the box with a lid.
6 After a week, feed the worms small amounts of food scraps placed under the damp newspaper, and then keep feeding the worms small amounts of food scraps every day.
7 Keep the soil damp but not soggy.
8 When enough liquid fertilizer has dripped into the tray, mix it with lots of water and pour around plants.

> The paper keeps the worms damp. The lid keeps out rainwater, sunlight, and pests.

How to make a simple compost heap

1 Pile up lawn clippings and leaves in a shaded area.
2 Mix the clippings and leaves with about the same amount of soil.
3 Mix in more soil if you add more clippings and leaves later.
4 Leave for three months to decompose.
5 Use the compost to fertilize the garden.

Decomposition timeline

This timeline shows how long it takes for products and materials to break down and return to the soil when left exposed to air and sunlight.

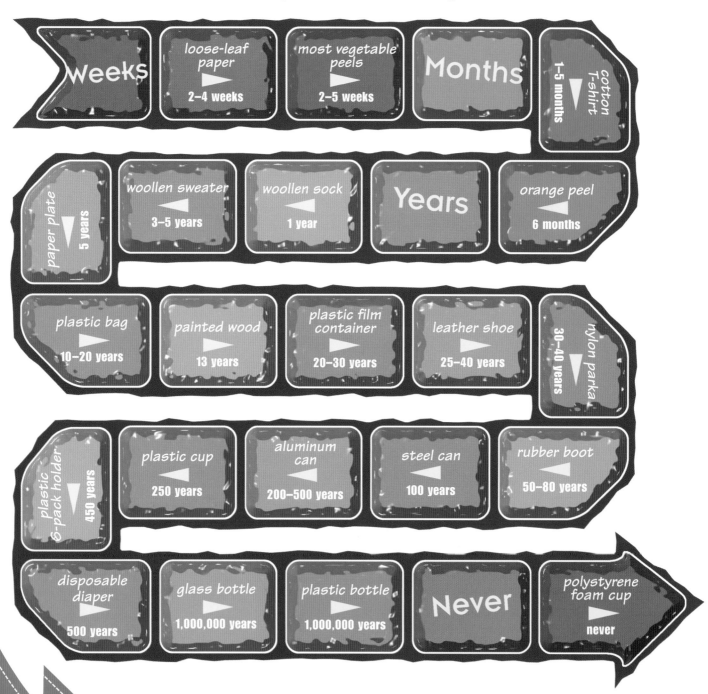

Weeks

loose-leaf paper
▶
2–4 weeks

most vegetable peels
▶
2–5 weeks

Months

cotton T-shirt
▼
1–5 months

paper plate
▼
5 years

woollen sweater
◀
3–5 years

woollen sock
◀
1 year

Years

orange peel
◀
6 months

plastic bag
▶
10–20 years

painted wood
▶
13 years

plastic film container
▶
20–30 years

leather shoe
◀
25–40 years

nylon parka
▼
30–40 years

plastic 6-pack holder
▼
450 years

plastic cup
◀
250 years

aluminum can
◀
200–500 years

steel can
◀
100 years

rubber boot
◀
50–80 years

disposable diaper
▶
500 years

glass bottle
▶
1,000,000 years

plastic bottle
▶
1,000,000 years

Never

polystyrene foam cup
▶
never

Glossary

acid rain rain containing dissolved industrial air pollution, which damages the environment

bacteria tiny living things that break down organic matter by eating it

carbon dioxide a gas breathed out by people and animals and taken in by trees, and also released by burning fossil fuels

compost decomposed plant and food waste, which is used to fertilize soil

contaminated ruined by harmful material; rainwater in landfills can be contaminated by poisonous substances in some plastics

decompose to break down into simple substances through the activity of tiny living organisms called bacteria

developed countries countries where most people have good living conditions and use a lot of manufactured products

fertilize to add decomposed material to the soil to improve plant growth

fossil fuels fuels, such as petroleum, coal, and natural gas, which formed from the remains of ancient plants and animals

global warming warming of the Earth's atmosphere due to the build-up of heat-holding gases

habitats areas where particular plants and animals live and breed

hydro-electric power electric power produced by a strong flow of water

inorganic fertilizers food for plants made from minerals taken from the ground

landfills large holes in the ground in which waste materials are buried

methane a gas released by burning fossil fuels, and decomposing organic waste and paper

natural resources materials taken from the Earth and used to make products, such as bauxite used to make aluminum

non-renewable cannot be made or grown again

organic waste waste material that was once living plant or animal matter, including food and plant waste

pollution dirty or harmful waste material that damages air, water, or land

pulped turned into a soggy mix of water and small, solid particles; paper is pulped before it is recycled

pure streams lots of items made of exactly the same material

raw materials materials that have not been processed or treated before, such as sand mined from beaches, sand dunes, and ocean beds

refining purifying or improving the quality of a raw material taken from the Earth

renewable can be made or grown again

reprocessing plant a factory where used household waste is made into new products

smelting melting alumina to separate out and remove the aluminum it contains

smog a brown-yellow haze that forms over industrial cities (**sm**oke and f**og**)

toxic poisonous

volume the amount of space something takes up

worm farms containers in which worms turn food scraps into organic fertilizer

Index